Portland is Weird:

The Official Unofficial Guide to the City's Uniqueness

An OPEN-ENDED DESTINATIONS Book

OPEN-ENDED DESTINATIONS

SPECIAL NOTE

If you would like any additional information about a particular item in this book, or would like to share comments/concerns/suggestions with any member of our team then please send an email to:
info@OpenEndedDestinations.com

ISBN: 1490578951
ISBN-13: 978-1490578958

CONTENTS

INTRODUCTION

Have you ever ridden your bike totally nude through the city streets with a thousand other naked people? Or ate dinner at a restaurant in complete darkness? Or went to a bookstore that handed out maps so you wouldn't get lost in the building? If you answered no to these questions then you have not truly experienced the uniqueness that is Portland, Oregon.

Open-Ended Destinations is proud to bring you an alternative look at Portland, the big city with the small town atmosphere that takes pride in being, well, weird. The team we assembled highlights the top twenty-five unique/weird/odd places in the Portland area and then lists an additional forty-six places, events, and things that didn't quite make the cut but were indeed all worthy of being a part of Portland's Finest Cornucopia of Weirdness.

Just like any city, Portland boasts a variety of different attractions including the basics such as: a zoo, museums, theaters, and breweries. However we delve into the more obscure to show you various ways that Portland stands out from the rest of the crowd. All the places listed in this book are not necessarily weird but through a collection of interviews and personal experiences we determined that people found these to be the most unique to this Pacific Northwestern town.

Open-Ended Destinations assembled a dynamic duo consisting of one Portland local and one out-of-town adventurer who visited Portland for the first time. The local is Chaz Terserton, the self-proclaimed third most eligible bachelor in Portland, Oregon and owner of the German Corgi named Klaus, who was the runner-up in the Pacific Northwest's Most Sophisticated Dog Bark Competition. The visitor is JoJo Apenan, the road tripper extraordinaire, who travels across the country in her custom-made Hobbit RV after she struck it rich with her book series about cavemen magicians.

Armed with Polaroid cameras, our team took to the streets to get a raw look at the eccentricities of Portland. Their goal was to gain different perspectives of the city so that this book could be beneficial on a few different levels. This is a guidebook for Portland visitors who have no doubt heard how weird this city is, so we've tried to highlight an array of these hotspots. You'll have at least a few stories to tell your families back home because we definitely don't want you to leave empty handed. And yet we also tried to include an assortment of events and lesser known places that would appeal to the year-round seasoned resident who is looking to have some oddly good times.

So without further ado, let's delve into the weirdness by asking these questions. Where else can you find Vegan Free-Range Christmas trees? Or catch a glimpse of the Unipiper, a unicycle riding Scotsman who dresses up as anything from Darth Vader, Gandalf, or one of the Mario Brothers as he rides around the city streets playing a bagpipe? A place where it's actually illegal to pump your own gas? A place that is one of the rainiest states in the country, yet the residents still take pride in not using umbrellas? A place where you can play in the snow in the mountains during the morning and then drive to the beach to watch the sunset and go swimming? A place where oddballs are celebrated?

Sit back, relax, and enjoy the weirdness dear reader, it's about to get kooky.

PORTLAND IS WEIRD

1. PORTLAND'S LIVING ROOM

Pioneer Courthouse Square

701 SW 6th Avenue
Public Space so Open 24/7

What better place to start than at the part of the city that's known as Portland's living room? If you are new to Portland or just visiting, this is one of the first places you will want to seek out. Not only is it a hub of downtown activities and events, but it is home to a visitor center filled with a goldmine of information.

There's something for everyone here at Pioneer Courthouse Square. Whether you're looking to witness your first Pigeon Royal Rumble, take a picture of a crazy street sign (pictured), or play a game of chess against one of the local congenial homeless men. But the best part of this square is that you get to hang out with your local Portlandians (or Portlanders as some call them).

This is by far one of the best places in the city for people watching, as it seems every type of person in Portland likes to pass through the living room at one point or another. On some days you might be just lucky enough to get a glimpse of them all. The outspoken yuppie echoing words of disdain towards the government from his perch on the amphitheater steps, the emo teenager passing out free hugs, or the carefree love-childs dipping their feet in the cool fountain water. On a nice day this place is humming with people from all walks of life.

Throughout the year, Pioneer Courthouse Square showcases a multitude of festivities including a farmer's market, beer festival, flower showcase, jazz concert and even a sand castle building competition. It also is home to the city's official Christmas tree, where sometimes over 300 tuba players come to play the commencement for the initial lighting of the holiday season.
Take a gander at the ground too as most of the bricks are personalized by donating citizens, including bricks with the names such as Mr. Spock and Bilbo Baggins.

2. PARK IN THE GUINNESS BOOK OF RECORDS

Mill Ends Park

Located in the median at the intersection of SW Taylor St and SW Naito
Pkwy
Open Daily 24/7 – Free

If you're looking for a place that has shattered records then just head over to Taylor Street where you can see the beauty of Mill Ends Park; it's in the Guinness Book of World Records as the World's Smallest City Park. Oh and it's also home to leprechauns. Don't believe us? Just take a look at the adjacent plaque on the corner of the street.

This park may be small (around 20 inches in diameter) but you never know what you might witness upon visiting. Sometimes the park is habituated by a squad of plastic army men, or a swimming pool for butterflies, and sometimes even a mini Ferris wheel. But if you're lucky you might be like the founder of this park and happen upon the park's head leprechaun, Patrick O'Toole. Many a newspaper articles have been written about the life and times of this specific leprechaun who established a colony in this perfectly sized piece of land.

The City of Portland has thrown many events for this beloved bit of nature, including St. Patrick's Day parties and an intense snail race. In regards to the aforementioned miniscule Ferris wheel, the city threw a huge ceremony involving using a full sized crane to put the Ferris wheel in the park. There is even a record of someone getting arrested at this park.

In April of 2013, a British Spokesperson has claimed that a park in London should overthrow the Mill Ends Park in the record book, sparking a battle of words and wits between the Brits and representatives from the Portland Parks and Recreation division. At the time of this publication, rest assured that Mill Ends Park still holds the title, sitting proudly on its throne for all to see, though be careful to keep your eyes open when crossing the street because you might just step right on it.

.

3. DOUGHNUTS A LA WEIRD

Voodoo Doughnuts

22 SW 3rd Avenue
Open 24/7 except on major holidays

When you listen to your Eminem albums do you always wish that there was some sort of Eminem themed donut to enjoy with the beats? We're not quite sure if that's what the owners of Voodoo Doughnuts had in mind when they first brainstormed this mouth-watering establishment, but we don't care, we are just glad this place exists. I'm sure if you told your friends you were going to Portland you heard at least one or two: "Dude you have to go to Voodoo." And yes dudes you really do need to check this place out even if you still happen to be in the midst of your New Year's Resolution Diet.

Captain My Captain. Voodoo Doll (pictured above). Diablos Rex. Marshall Mathers. Cock-N-Balls. How can you possibly go wrong with doughnut names such as these? Though they are quite delicious, this place really isn't about the taste but more of just the experience and being able to mention to someone that you had a doughnut with Cap N' Crunch on it. And yes it even comes equipped with a rotating display case to show off their wild assortment of doughy delectables.

So go for the ambiance or for the creativity of the donuts or simply to stuff your face with some tasty treats, but a trip to Portland is not complete until you've visited Voodoo Doughnuts. Just make sure you bring some cash because they don't accept anything else. And a word of caution, many people flock to this place so if you venture over during peak hours you will be met with an extremely long line wrapping around the outside of the building.

There are three Voodoo stores currently operating but the one on 3rd Avenue is the mother ship.

4. THE MOST BREEZY BIKE RIDE
YOU WILL EVER GO ON

World Naked Bike Ride

1219 SW Park Avenue
June 8th, 2013

Yes, this event is exactly what it sounds like. It's a bike ride. In the nude. If you haven't noticed yet, Portland may be obsessed with roses, but it also seems to be obsessed with nudity. Maybe it's just because most Portlandians are comfortable with whom they are, and they like the feeling of being not only free-spirited but free-bodied as well. Regardless of the reasons, this event is truly exciting but only platonically.

So why would anyone want to ride a bicycle through city streets with a group consisting of thousands of naked people? Well, there are actually quite many different reasons that people participate including: to raise awareness for the safety of bike rides, to protest the growing extreme use of pollution-based transport, to promote body awareness and being comfortable in your skin, and of course many people just do it to have fun and a new experience.

The Portland Art Museum supports this cause by opening its doors for the riders before the actual race. Admission prices are dependent on the amount of clothing you are wearing as they charge one dollar per piece of clothing. And even though this would seem like something of a dirty event because of all the nudity, in fact it is quite the opposite. Many locals LOVE this event and claim it gives them such a sense of family and camaraderie with their fellow Portland residents. If you witness this event it would be hard to argue with this as everyone seems so genuinely happy throughout the ride and so nice and pleasant with one another. Since it is an organized protest it is not illegal either, as the Portland Police Department has become fully involved in clearing the streets and providing an escort for the group.

One year the city had 7,000 participants, officially making Portland the Naked Bicycling Capital of the World. So go ahead and take it off, take it all off.

5. MUSEUM INTO THE SEVENTH DIMENSION

The Faux Museum: Gallery & Store

139 NW 2nd Avenue
Tues-Sat Noon-7pm   Sun Noon-5pm

A long time ago, long before the technology rush birthed by the human race, there lived a majestic creature that roamed the lands. This creature was known as the Woolly Ant. Long thought to be extinct, historians were forced to rewrite the history books as the sole survivor of this unique species climbed its way back out into the spotlight. As if by some kind of fate, this weird creature now resides in the city of Portland, at the Faux Museum on 2nd Avenue.

If you are looking for a museum that best captures the "weirdness" of Portland then this is definitely the place you want to check out. The Faux Museum is a museum filled with oddity, wonder, and a lot of inventive and amusing art exhibitions. It claims to be the first and oldest museum in the entire world, dating back to over 10,000 years ago. Don't believe me? The first part of the interactive tour features a history of the Faux family, with detailed descriptions of those involved as well as massive maps depicting the path that led them to Portland.

It would be unfair to give too much information about the exhibits, as experiencing them on your own with virgin ears and eyes makes the visit so much more entertaining. But let's just say that upon entering its like stepping inside the Twilight Zone, complete with cardboard and blanket constructed walls and pathways, videos of random sporadic video clips and sound bites, and a journey into the 7th Dimension. A place to help change your way of life, as well as to learn the true power and love of the hedgehog. After the self-guided tour you are free to spin the wheel of prizes and roam the gift shop of oddities. Sitting behind the extremely ancient cash register is your host and friend, Tom, who will be happy to give you all the information you need to know about the exhibits or life in general. New exhibits are put in a few times a year, and as of 2013 the price is $6. Or even better, admission on your birthday is only $1.

6. THE SLEEPING GIANT

Mount Hood

About 50 miles East of Portland

You may be asking yourself why we have added a piece of landscape to a book focusing on oddities. What's special about a mountain? Every city in the country seems to have their own special mountain, right? Not like this. Not like Mount Hood. There is nothing weird about Mt. Hood, but it's like the city's guardian angel; not quite close enough to be too overpowering but always easily seen off in the distance watching over us. And a few interesting tidbits make this mountain just as unique as the city it guards.

For starters, Mt Hood is a sleeping giant. It is a volcano, a potentially active volcano. The last documented eruption was back in 1907 but experts claim that the chance of it erupting within the next thirty years is significant. It's like the dreaded "boy band," you know another prefabricated one is going to emerge and sweep the nation but you hope and pray it doesn't happen in your lifetime. And just like boy bands, Mt Hood spews a lot of hot steam through various cracks in its walls. If you look hard enough you may just find a hot spring or two as well.

But don't let the thought of hot molten lava scare you away, as this mountain is perfect for the outdoor lover. It's a great place to hike, camp, bike, ski, or climb. In fact, according to statistics, it is one of the most climbed mountains in the world. Mt. Hood also boasts the only area in North America where there is year round skiing.

Yes, you could go skiing in the morning and then drive to the nearby Oregon coast and go surfboarding in the ocean in the very same day. So if you are visiting Portland in mid-summer, take a trip up to the Timberline Lodge Ski Area and surprise your friends with a photo of yourself playing in the snow in your bathing suit. Or you can just do like the guy in the above photo and go in your birthday suit.

7. A COFFEE HOUSE
FIT FOR THE TWILIGHT ZONE

Rimsky-Korsakoffee House

707 SE 12th Avenue
Sun-Thu 7pm-12am Fri-Sat 7pm-1am

You probably won't hear this statement uttered many times throughout your life but… you HAVE to check out this bathroom. There are dozens and dozens of coffee houses and cafes sprawled throughout the Portland area and many of them are unique and serve a delicious cup of joe, but Rimsky-Korsakoffee House is the one that truly captures the weirdness and eccentricity of the Portland culture. It's definitely one of those places you can tell your family back home about and they'll confirm what most of the nation believes: Portland is weird.

Just the fact that the owners turned a colonial residential house into their own little coffee house sets it apart from the others. The ambiance is quirky, with its various sized tables and miss matched wooden antique chairs. Purple and orange Christmas lights line the corners of the walls, shining a warm glow onto the dining area. Random trinkets hang from the dining room ceiling: a dollar bill, a picture of Shrek, a plastic orange peel…

Hidden gems are abound in this house that is both warm and inviting, yet weird and creepy. A few of the tables rotate ever so slightly in a circle so if you're not careful you may reach down and drink from your neighbor's cup. Vintage china sets are used to serve their drinks and exquisite selection of desserts. The hint of a face can be seen in the wallpaper, almost as if a spirit is trying to break free from the captivity of the wall. Sometimes you are graced with the elegant classical music from a live person playing the piano that's in the corner and other times you are entertained with pre-recorded music that sounds like a mixture of 50's Big Band music, a theme from black and white horror movies, with a dash of French ambiance instruments.

Side note: Cash only. But seriously, check out the bathroom. It is freaky.

8. A RACE FIT FOR A KING…
OR POSSIBLY THE JESTER

Adult Soap Box Derby Races at Mt. Tabor

SE 60th Avenue
August 17th, 2013

Have you ever wanted to build your own boxcar from scratch and race it down the side of a volcano? Well then in Portland you could make your dreams come true! Don't fret, the volcano is extinct but the dangers are still real in the Portland Adult Soap Box Derby. Every year, since 1997, teams of creative geniuses build their own themed soapbox cars and adorn themselves in their best outfits/costumes to compete in a winding, fast-paced downhill race on the roads of Mt. Tabor in Northeast Portland. Mt. Tabor in itself is a unique addition to the Portland culture as it is one of the country's first parks to be built on an extinct volcano.

It's interesting to see how the different teams approach this race, as some go for intriguing aero-dynamic and engineer intensive designs, while others seem bent on constructing the most outlandish and ornamental design regardless of whether it'll make it all the way down the hill or not. To accommodate these aspiring artists/entertainers, awards are given for not only speed and engineering categories but also art and crowd pleasure awards. Some past soapboxes include a Giant Weiner Dog, a Beer Garden and multiple cars with water gun armed drivers.

The beauty of this yearly event is that it's done purely for the fun and creativity of it. Everyone involved are volunteers, including the people that created and run it every year. There is no cost to watch and you can bring your own food and beer. This is a free event, but a word of caution: it's rapidly becoming a must see event in Portland and thousands flock to witness its glory every year. So beware of heavy traffic and limited parking spots. But the spectacle is well worth these little hassles, and you can even make a day of it by bringing coolers and picnics to celebrate with the entire family. Enter if you dare, or just come down to cheer on your favorite rider as there is sure to be plenty of worthy sightseeing.

9. THE MOST BIZARRE STORE IN PORTLAND

Freakybuttrue Peculiarium

2234 NW Thurman Street
Wed, Thurs, Fri 11am-5pm Sat 11am-7pm Sun 11am-5pm

Sasquatch is alive and well, and he's currently living near the entrance of a place called Freakybuttrue Peculiarium. Just the name of this place was enough reason to add it to this book, but it is more than just a boastful name. It is part gag store, part dare-eating café, and part oddity museum. The word "weird" cannot be used to describe this place as it is on a whole other level. Perhaps the term far out is better fitting. Or eccentric. One might even say that it is just downright, flat-out, completely bizarre.

The museum portion of this store is small but manages to fit as assortment of freakiness into its confines; plus it is free so it is definitely worth a visit. The museum is home to things such as Al Capone's actual personal house safe, as well as an exhibit on human spontaneous combustion. There is also a neon-glow room (pictured above) with a sink full of markers that you are free to use on anything and everything in the room.

The store portion features interesting (and yes freaky) pieces of art work and various antique items including an old rotary phone. Gag gifts are another key component to the store and you're sure to find an item or two to make you laugh or take home as a souvenir. There is also a photo op section revolving around a group of aliens clearly having too much fun dissecting a human being.

And if that wasn't enough for you, then swing by the little eatery inside and try out one of their desserts. You'll be happy to know they have freaky specialty desserts too, featuring, amongst other things, sundaes topped with maggots. Yes real maggots. If you're man (or woman) enough to choke down these tasty treats, you'll get your picture taken and officially be added to the Insectarian Club.

10. BOOKSTORE ON STEROIDS

Powell's City of Books

1005 W Burnside Street
Open Daily from 9am-11pm

Any lover of literature will tell you that they could get lost in a bookstore for hours, but Powell's City of Books is one of the few national bookstores that you could literally get lost in for long periods of time. It's the world's largest independent bookstore. One of the places that truly identifies with the city of Portland. And yes, they do hand out actual maps to aid you in your quest to find the perfect book, as well as to save them from having to send out a search party for you.

If you travel to Portland without visiting Powell's then you have truly not visited Portland. I mean c'mon who doesn't love books? But regardless of whether you're a book nerd or not, this store needs to be visited solely based on its mammoth size. Here are a few fun facts to whet your appetite:

Occupies an entire full square block of the city.
68,000 square feet
1.6 acres of retail floor space
1.5 million books spread through nine color-coded rooms

One of the best characteristics about this bookstore is that its shelves are filled with both brand new books as well as very reasonably priced used books. If there is a particular book you are searching for, then you can almost rest assure it's physically on the shelves at Powell's. This location also contains a "Rare Books Room" that houses some interesting finds.

So take a stroll around the floors. Or just grab a map as a souvenir. But make sure you at least visit Powell's City of Books if you want to call yourself a true Portlandian.

11. NO NEED TO PRAY OR LOVE WHEN THERE IS ALL THIS FOOD TO EAT

The Portland Food Carts

Located throughout City but this Particular Row is on 5th Avenue at Stark Street

The city of Portland is serious about their food carts. Very. Serious.

Within a matter of fifty feet, you have the opportunity of choosing from a delectable assortment of food. Whether you are in the mood for Mediterranean, Asian, Czech, German, Korean, Mexican, or American food, really is something for everyone.

You could pick out twenty random people on the streets and ask them what their favorite Food Cart is and you will most assuredly get at least twelve different answers, and a variety of reasons as to why that particular one is Portland's Best. It really depends on what type of food you are craving and what street you happen to be on that day. But if you're new, here's a few of our favorites to get you started.

If you are a lover of grilled cheese and burgers then you definitely need to head on down to the BrunchBox on 5th Avenue. This cart substitutes full grilled cheese sandwiches for the buns that they use on the burgers. Just ask for the Redonkadonk. Also, as of this publication, if you check in on Foursquare they will give you fifty percent off your order. The Frying Scotsman, featuring a delectable variety of fish, is another one of our favorites, as well as the favorite of many people in the city. I mean c'mon who doesn't love some deep fried fish?

Like Pioneer Square, this is a perfect spot for people watching. Just sitting on a nearby bench for under an hour, you'll have a chance to view all that the city has to offer. Tattoo covered teenagers standing next to old men decked out in suits. Check. Guy with a backpack full of arrows sticking out of it. Check. Woman flying a kite the size of a postage stamp. Check. Guy sitting on the sidewalk playing a keyboard while singing about Irish women. Check. A group of twenty people walking by taking a tour and flashing their cameras at everything they see. Check.

12. A BIG PART OF PORTLAND HISTORY

Pittock Mansion

3229 NW Pittock Drive
Tours Open from 11am-4pm, Grounds Open from 6am-9pm

Travel on up Pittock Drive and you will be met by two different amazing views. The first is an absolutely stunning house with accompanying extravagant garden. The second is a view of downtown Portland. The consensus around Portland is that this is one of the best photo-opportunistic spots to capture the city's skyline: a breathtaking view through a frame of trees and a backdrop of the snow-blanketed peaks of Mt. Hood. If you have ever come across a photograph of a beautiful picture of downtown Portland from a high vantage point, then there's a ninety percent chance that picture came from this spot.

This view of Portland is on the backside of the mansion's landscape and is free to the public, as is the rest of the garden area and paths around the property. Come for the view of the city, but stay for the views of this monstrosity of a house. This 46-acre, 16,000 square foot, 44 room mansion was built in 1914 and home to Henry Pittock, hence the name of the mansion and adjacent street. It even came equipped with an intercom system, an elevator, and a personalized shower that would make even present day people jealous.

Though it was originally built for private use, the inside of the mansion is now open to the public for tours and private events. (There is a fee involved for the tour. There are also public restrooms on site.) And if you are in the area around the Christmas season, this is definitely a good time to tour the inside as it will be decorated to the max in holiday cheer.

Pittock Mansion is a great way to spend the afternoon; you could hike up a path in the Forest Park and make an outdoor adventure of it; or pack a lunch, drive up to their free parking area, and have a picnic at one of their benches overlooking the West Hills 1,000 feet below. Whether you want to take the inside tour or not, this is definitely an intricate part of Portland to visit.

13. GAMES FOR REAL MEN

Portland Highland Games

26000 SE Stark Street
July 20th, 2013

You don't have to be Scottish to enjoy the Portland Highland Games, but just remember there will be kilts involved. A lot of kilts.

On the third week of July, at Mt. Hood Community College in Gresham, you have a chance to walk into a little piece of Scotland only a stone's throw from downtown Portland.

You haven't seen a real man until you watch one in a kilt toss a telephone pole while barely breaking a sweat. This festival, that has been going on for over 60 years now, features a variety of activities including: a Kilted mile race, a parade of clans, sheepdog demonstrations, whiskey tasting sessions, Scottish country dancing, and tug of war. In addition to those spectacles, highly skilled adults (and youths) duke it out in competitions ranging from bagpiping and drumming, to dancing and fiddling.

The campus is also loaded with booths full of goodies and arts and crafts.

From the looks of the events and articles in this book it seems as if many are geared towards adults, especially with all the nudity and/or alcoholic beverages involved, but the Portland Highland Games is a fantastic event to be enjoyed by the whole family. There are even kids participating in some of the competitions throughout this festival.

So whether you're looking for some educational experiences, looking to see tough men in kilts show off their skills, or just looking for a good time then head on over to the Portland Highland Games and do your best Shrek impersonation.

This is not a free event so buy tickets ahead of time online or make sure to bring plenty of cash.

14. PUT A HAT ON IT

The Hat Museum

1928 SE Ladd Avenue
Open Year Round from 10am-6pm but Reservations are Required
(503) 232-0433

With over a 1,000 hats this establishment is clearly America's Largest Hat Museum. Seems only fitting that a rainy place like Portland would have such a massive collection of hats.

Nestled on a beautiful tree-covered street, at the end of a block of quaint houses in eastern Portland, The Hat Museum is a three floored Victorian house packed to the brim with fancy and sophisticated hats of all kinds. The people in charge take great pride in their collection of hats, and their passion shines through brightly during the tour when they detail quite a vast knowledge and interesting tidbits about the hats and about Portland history in general.

There is a wide variety of hat collections, ranging from international hats, to antique and vintage hats, as well as rooms full of fun and unusual headwear. And just in case you are bit by the hat bug, at the end of the tour you can browse the gift shop in order to find the perfect hat to purchase for your very own collection.

Call ahead before showing up and bring money with you because the museum is not free, but the admission price includes the private educational tour as well as a discount at the gift shop.

15. A GATHERING PLACE FOR ROSES FROM AROUND THE WORLD

International Rose Test Garden

400 SW Kingston Avenue
Open Daily from 7:30am-9pm

Why don't you stop and smell the roses? Whether you want to take this quote literally or figuratively, this is one of the best and definitely the most unique place to accomplish this in Portland. During its peak months, if you are even within a block of this garden you will be able to smell the roses.

How many flowers would you say are in a good sized garden? 100? 1,000? Well seeing as Portland is known as the "City of Roses" everyone should have known that they weren't going to take their Rose Garden lightly. This beautiful garden is blanketed with about 10,000 rosebushes!

Some of the other attractions to this park include the Miniature Rose Garden as well as the Shakespeare Garden. On the east side of the garden is an outdoor amphitheater consisting of towering bushes standing in place of the curtains and a tiered grandstand complete with grass seats. This is a perfect place to relax or get in some reading, and you're sure to spot a young Romeo and Juliet wrapped in a lover's embrace either on the stage or the lush grass beneath it.

But one word of caution, these are not fake plants and it can get rather cold in Portland during the winter months so don't expect to see roses year round. If you come in the winter you will not see anything blooming, but it's still a beautiful and clean park to relax in with great skyline views of downtown Portland and the luminous Mount Hood. If you are specifically looking to see the roses then your best bet is to travel to the garden in the months of mid-May to August. You will not be disappointed. As the plaque of William Shakespeare says in his respective part of the garden, "Of all flowers methinks a rose is best."

And the best part of this garden besides the roses? The garden is completely free of charge.

16. IT'S GOOD TO BE A KID, ESPECIALLY WHEN YOU'RE AN ADULT

Ground Kontrol

511 NW Couch Street
Open Daily from Noon-2:30am

Break open that change jar and gather all the quarters you can find and then throw caution to the wind (as well as your laundry) and head on down to Ground Kontrol for hours of fun. If nostalgia is what you are looking for then this place has got it. Ground Kontrol is basically an interactive museum of the history of the public gaming systems, and with cool neon-lighted bathrooms that transport you into Tron.

This is an arcade for adults, with its accompanying full bar and beer holders attached to almost every game so you don't have to worry about spilling any precious liquid from your glass as you intensely battle to defeat the pixelated boss of level three.

Not exactly an arcade for the young as they will most undoubtedly ridicule the horrible graphics and be bored with the two-buttoned control systems and one-dimensional storylines. But these games are sure to thrill anyone that grew up in the early 90s and earlier. And if pinball is your vice then head up to the second floor where the walls are lined with over a dozen differently themed pinball machines.

The café portion of this arcade features neon tables, a movie projection screen, and the aforementioned full bar wrought with happy hour drinks and interesting food choices such as the peanut butter and marshmallow sandwich. Ground Kontrol also holds many events including: RockBand competitions, Terminator Costume & Challenge Night, Metal Mondays, and on certain nights they have a 5 dollar cover charge but then you get to play any games as long as you like for free. There is no cover charge on the rest of the nights but if you are going to show up in the evening on any night, make sure you bring your ID because you will get carded at door.

17. AMERICA'S BICYCLE MECCA

Pedalpalooza

Throughout The City and the Suburbs
June 6-29th, 2013

Two hundred and fifty. That's the number most associated with Pedalpalooza, the yearly bike event that takes place in the city of Portland. And it's not referring to the number of bike riders involved; it's the number of bike RIDES associated with this event. Yes, over the span of three straight weeks, Pedalpalooza features over 250 differently themed bicycle rides! No wonder Portland is referred to as America's Bicycle Mecca.

It's not just a bunch of boring old rides repeated over and over; in fact it's a smorgasbord of creatively imagined rides that are sure to make even the hardest of souls smile a little. Some of the rides are intense and extreme but most of the rides are just plain fun, and almost every single one of them is free to participate in. Here are a few of the rides just to give you an idea of some of the weirdness that encompasses Pedalpalooza:

Fake Mustache Ride – Bike around in your best fake mustache and make the rest of the city jealous. Star Wars vs. Star Trek – Dress up as your favorite character and then duel it out against the lesser space-aged creatures through the use of squirt guns and water balloons. Tree Hugger's Ride – Ride to a few different parks to hug trees and dance around them while singing. There are even educational rides/workshops including ones that teach you how to repair any part of your bike, and another one that teaches you how to ride a unicycle. You don't even have to have your own unicycle, because they provide them for you. Just make sure you bring some safety gear.

Whether you like to ride your bicycle in costume, or in a suit and top hat, or even completely naked, you are sure to find similar folks in Portland to accompany you on your ride.

18. PORTLAND'S SPIRITUAL SANCTUARY

The Grotto

NE 85th Avenue and NE Sandy Boulevard
Opens Daily at 9am, Closes between 5pm-8pm Depending on Season

Tucked along the busy streets of the east, is a quiet nature sanctuary shrouded in religious energy. The Grotto is an internationally-renowned Catholic sanctuary and garden, but one does not need to be Catholic, nor even religious, to visit and enjoy this place of solitude and peace.

Near the parking lot you have the option of walking through the Stations of the Cross, a nature path with rock alters depicting each station of the cross. This is a great spot for peaceful tranquility and quiet reflection as the path winds through a mix of ferns, moss, vines and massive towering "angel" trees.

Deeper down into the property is the Grotto, which is an alter built directly into the side of an impressive towering cliff. A statue of the Mother Mary holding Jesus in her arms is the centerpiece of this enclave and down the stone steps are rows of wooden pews amidst the trees. The lower plaza level is free to the public, but there is a charge of a few dollars if you want to ride the elevator to the top of the cliff. This is an impressive free standing cement elevator shaft that climbs the side of the cliff to take you to the gardens on the vista. Upon reaching the top level you are free to roam the beautiful gardens and look out onto views of the city down below.

The ground level also houses an actual brick and mortar church, the Chapel of Mary, which performs masses for the public on a daily basis. An outdoor mass amidst the towering trees and cliff is performed during the summers at noon on Sundays. The Grotto is also home to the Festival of Lights every Christmas season.

The Grotto is a perfect spot to reenergize the positive feelings in your body and soul, a place to quietly reflect on your life.

19. THE PLACE TO BE ON SATURDAY MORNING

Portland Saturday Market

Located at the Tom McCall Waterfront Park near Burnside Bridge
Sat 10am-5pm   Sun 11am-4:30pm

Rain or shine, Portland's Saturday Market is the place to be on weekend mornings in the downtown Portland area.

Contrary to what the name suggests, this market operates on Sunday too. Every Saturday and Sunday throughout the year (except for January and February) over 250 artists/vendors assemble to bring you a wide taste of Portland into one little hub right next to the waterfront. Because of the city wide embracement of odd people, Portland is thriving with creativity on many levels. The Portland Saturday Market is a great place to experience this eclectic creativity of the city in one neatly packaged place. Artists and craftsmen of all walks of life, flock to the market to showcase their labors of love to the masses.

In addition to all the booths and exhibits, this market features live music near the fountain and on nicer days you are sure to run into a few street performers that put on shows with a mixture of juggling, magic, and comedy. Even though the area is usually packed, there's a great sense of community between everyone which factors into quite a happy environment.

This isn't your daddy's weekend market; this is not a community yard sale full of random junk. This market attracts some of Portland's most unique and creative entrepreneurs who try to dazzle you with their artistic endeavors. This is a fantastic place to do some gift shopping, especially for people looking for gifts that capture the quirkiness of Portland.

And make sure you eat an elephant ear while you're there, they are quite tasty.

20. A POTENTIALLY LIFE-CHANGING EXPERIENCE

The Blind Café

2800 SE Harrison Street
Advanced Tickets Must Be Purchased

Have you ever eaten a meal in pitch darkness? The Blind Café offers something totally unique, and it's not just a one-trick gimmick to attract curious money baggers, but this concept is for a noble and noteworthy cause. It's not just a novelty cool meal, it is an experience. Many people have walked away from this event with a little more self-discovery and some have even shed a tear or two.

Picture this: sitting in complete darkness with your group as you place your order with the blind wait staff, and then eating your meal without even being able to see what is on the plate in front of you! The idea behind the Blind Café is to raise awareness towards the blind, as well as raise money to help fund the group that raises puppies to become seeing-eye dogs for the blind. The experience also acts as a way for people to get in touch with their own lives and feelings, as they are forced to rely on their other senses and, through a different vantage point, partake in an activity that most people take for granted.

The Blind Café is a specialty dinner that only runs on certain days of the year and requires a ticket purchase to be a part of this rare event. The tickets range from $45-$95 but include a multitude of things such as: two hours in total darkness accompanied by original live music, a sensory enhanced dining experience, and a unique discussion period with the blind wait staff. A portion of the proceeds also go towards helping out the blind community in Portland.

It is truly a unique experience and boasts yet another reason why people claim that in Portland the most important thing is the community. The Blind Café is not just a great way to connect with the family you share the dinner with but also a wonderful way to connect with yourself.

21. YET ANOTHER REASON TO OWN A BIKE IN PORTLAND

Zoobomb

West Hills – Washington Park
Sunday Nights

This weekly event has nothing to do with bombs and nothing to do with zoos, other than the fact that the starting point is in the vicinity of the zoo. For over a decade now, the fun loving citizens of Portland have taken their bikes to the street for a weekly night joy ride. There is nothing sinister or delinquent about this bike race, in fact many people claim that the purpose of it is to support bicycle advocacy and a safe community. Though there is nothing wrong with participating just for the pure fun of it.

Zoobomb entails riding your bike through the streets of the West Hills, starting up on the ground level of the Washington Park MAX station. It's not really a race per say, especially since upon reaching the finish line most people get right on the MAX and head back up to the beginning to do it all over again.

This started out over a decade ago with just a small group of people having some fun, and it initially was met with some backlash from the community and authorities. But over the years it has formed into a city pastime and has even been condoned by the mayor. Though some weeks still only pull in a small group of people, at times during the summer it wouldn't be rare to spot hundreds of participators cycling down the hills in bikes of all shapes and sizes. Weird and unique bikes are encouraged as well as the riders dressing in costumes or their coolest gear.

And if you are visiting and don't have a bike? Well, pictured above is the Zoobomb monument which contains a bundle of bikes that people can borrow to use for the ride. It seems like the citizens of Portland are always looking out for one another.

22. NOT YOUR TYPICAL DINER

The Roxy Diner

1121 SW Stark Street
Open 24 Hours Tues-Sun Closed on Mondays

This bustling little diner in the Glamour District has seen the likes of Cheech and Chong to Siegfried and Roy. No, not the actual celebrities, but entrees named for these famous people and many more. Upon entering The Roxy you are met with an eclectic assortment of décor ranging from Star Wars, to Quentin Tarantino, Elvis, babies in crowns, and a life-size crucifix of Jesus hanging above the ever playing jukebox.

It's a place filled with leopard print chairs. It's a place wrought with a mix of 70's and 80's music from the jukebox with a little hint of early 90s. Open twenty four hours a day, except for Mondays, it's a place that you can hang out at no matter what time of day it is and no matter what kind of condition you are in. On Monday this place is closed for nefarious reasons that you can find on the first page of their menu, a booklet filled with many puns and insults.

It's a Portland late-night hotspot so if you're looking to experience this dive without the crowds then you would do best to swing by in the early afternoon. That way you'll still have the opportunity to mingle with the occasional hipster or Goth, but it'll be slow enough to enjoy the ambiance and the excellent staff who are as eclectic as the décor.

But just so you know... there is NO ALCOHOL served so this is not a place to get your groove on, it's more of a place to recover from your groove. And if you bring kids just be aware that they may pose questions from things they read on the menu such as "Daddy what's a tranny?" or "Mommy what's this four letter F-word mean?"

Oh and if you ever wanted to look at a waiter with a straight face and say, "Sir I shall have the Poo Poo Platter," then this is the place you want to visit.

23. COSTUMES, SHOPPING CARTS, BEER… TIME TO RACE PORTLAND STYLE

Portland's Urban Iditarod

Hawthorne Bridge
February/March

Every year, the great state of Alaska holds one of the most intense and compelling races in the world. Dog sled teams race across the hazardous terrains of the frozen tundra, battling both the grueling emotional and physical hardships that are faced.

The city of Portland decided to emulate this majestic race but with its own Portlandian touch. Instead of sleds, Portland uses shopping carts. And instead of dogs, Portland uses creatively (sometimes) dressed people tied together with string to pull the shopping cart through the urban streets of the downtown area. Along the path are designated pit stops at local bars for the barking "dogs" to catch their breath and rehydrate their livers.

Though clearly not even a slight fraction of being as intense as the Alaskan version, come cheer on these souls that brave the brisk and rainy Portland winter air as they clad themselves in costumes for your viewing pleasure. Though the teams seek to win the race, they are also in a duel to see who can come up with the most creatively themed "sleds" and attire. These teams thrive off the attending audience so cheer on your favorite costumed team and have a beer with them at the finish line during the after party.

Though it costs money to enter the actual mushing, it is free to swing by and enjoy the sightseeing. If you are looking to sign up, make sure you do it early as the allotted number of teams is limited and they fill up fast. This event usually takes place in March though has hit the streets in February before too.

24. THE SCHOOL YOU'LL WANT TO ATTEND WHILE ON VACATION

McMenamins Kennedy School

5736 NE 33rd Avenue

Just because its summertime doesn't mean that school is out, in fact, in Portland one of the biggest summer hotspots is a school. The McMenamins are the kings of Oregon and their most unique and prized possession is the Kennedy School. But alas my friends do not fret for this particular school requires no exams and no books, and definitely no teacher's dirty looks. This school is an exclusive destination all wrapped into one antique school building.

The Kennedy School opened in 1915 but was forced to shut its doors in the summer of 1975 when repair costs reached a height that could not be achieved. In 1997, the McMenamins did an overhaul of the building and reopened it into what it is today. This school is now home to 35 guestrooms for lodging, a few different restaurants and bars, a brewery, a gift shop, a movie theater, and a warm saltwater soaking pool. It features all of these amenities yet still maintains the integrity of the original school.

All the creaky floored hallways are still there, the walls adorned with mementos and information about the history of the building. As well as the classrooms which have been turned into the 35 guest hotel rooms and feature the original chalkboards but are updated to include private baths and the likes. The Courtyard Restaurant is inside the school cafeteria and features an assortment of hanging décor as well as an outside courtyard dining area complete with fireplace and gardens.

It is truly one of Portland's most unique and interesting sites and it is a great place to take one of their self-guided tours even if you don't plan on staying for dinner or spending the night. Also, unlike many places in Portland, this spot has its own large, free parking lot.

25. THE FESTIVAL THAT CAPTURES THE CITY'S HEART AND SOUL

Portland Rose Festival

1020 SW Naito Parkway
May 19th-June 16th, 2013

Most cities in this country can be identified with a singular theme, for example: Los Angeles – movie stars, Chicago – wind, Phoenix – dry heat. And Portland has… roses. Lots and lots of roses. The city is obsessed with these delicate flowers. So it only seems natural that a town referred to as the "City of Roses" would also have a yearly event called the Portland Rose Festival. Every year, what seems like the entire population of Portland, descends to this world renowned festival that literally has something for everyone.

This festival has been going on for over a hundred years now, as the very first Rose Festival here happened back in 1907! It's located amidst the Tom McCall Waterfront, a beautiful park nestled in between the bustling skyscrapers and the flowing waters of the Willamette River. The festivities usually appear near the end of May/early June and run about three weeks or so depending on the events of that particular year.

The festivities start off with the Rock 'n' Roll Portland Half Marathon and culminates in an extravagant fireworks display. Spread over a few weeks, dozens of different activities and festivities are thrown in to make sure everyone has a good time. There are classic festival attractions such as carnival rides, food and game booths, and an exciting playlist of live musical concerts.

But the Portland Rose Festival takes it one step further by adding dozens of unique twists and events including: dragon boat races, floral parades, starlight runs, rose shows, soccer games, milk carton boat races, Rose Cup races, and many, many more. And yes there will be plenty of roses.

26. THE BEST OF THE REST – PLACES OF INTEREST

---- "Because who doesn't want a little King at 3 in the morning?"
24 Hour Church of Elvis
408 NW Couch Street
UPDATE The 24 Hour Church of Elvis currently does not have a physical location anymore, but funds are being raised to get this Portland landmark up and running again. Check them out online if you are interested.
If you asked a dozen different Portlandians what exactly is the 24 Hour Church of Elvis you'll probably get twelve different answers and none of them will be conclusive. It is part kitsch, part fortune tellers, part Barbie dolls, and a whole lot of weird and bizarre. Bring a handful of quarters with you because this beauty is fully coin-operated and is definitely a unique part of Portland's lore.

---- "Pi for everyone! Well except for the people who engraved this..."
If you get off the local MAX at the Washington Park Exit you will notice a variety of engravings in the granite walls. One of these being the math term "Pi" and it is quite impressive considering it is written out to 107 decimal places. There's just one tiny problem... they got the numbers wrong from the second line on. Oops.

---- "I must say, that dog was bound to his home."
Grave of Bobbie the Wonder Dog
1067 NE Columbia Avenue
This is the burial place of the famous scotch collie dog that traveled on his own, 2,500 miles from Indiana to Oregon after he got lost while he was with his owners on vacation. Six months after being lost, he showed back up at the front door of his home. Afterwards he became uber famous and even spawned shows and movies. The final resting place of this amazing dog is located at the Oregon Humane Society building and comes complete with a fancy well-to-do dog house near his headstone.

---- "Birds need libraries too right?"
The Little Free Library
7518 SW 36th Avenue
Throughout the Portland Metro area are at least a dozen strange, unique looking mailboxes/birdhouses but upon closer inspection you will become aware of another aspect that portrays the spirit of community in Portland. They are referred to as the Little Free Libraries and are exactly what they sound like. They are little miniature libraries situated on poles in front of normal residents' houses. Inside is an assortment of books that anyone walking by is allowed to borrow and read and then bring back to any of the locations. No library card or signing up necessary, it's all about good faith and promoting reading throughout the community. And bonus, the particular Little Library on 36th Avenue is shaped like a miniature TARDIS from the popular Doctor Who.

---- "Who says sugar can't make you look fabulous?!"
Sugar Me
131 NE Fremont Street
Make sure you stop on by Sugar Me if you are looking for something a little more tasteful. But don't let the name fool you because I'm not talking about candy. Yes, there is sugar involved but not in regards to eating it. It actually serves as a sweet way to wax off body hairs. Check out the company's website and Facebook to get coupons and deals off your visits. Many women can attest that this is definitely a less painful alternative to "getting your wax on." The staff is great, the procedure is simple, and the discomfort afterwards is miniscule… so head on over to Sugar Me and have yourself a treat.

---- "How much dirt is in a hole that is twenty feet deep and five feet wide?"
Woodstock Mystery Hole
Old Town Chinatown
Only the town of Portland would celebrate a hole that leads to nowhere and has nothing in it. This nationally famous hole is located in a privately owned backyard, and the owner delights in taking visitors on tours through this oddity. Just a heads up, finding this place is almost as much as a mystery as the hole itself. At the time of this publication, the tours are on a hiatus until further notice for personal reasons.

---- "Pull My Finger Statue"
Portlandia Statue
1120 SW 5th Avenue
Yes, some natives of Portland call this copper monument the "Pull My Finger Statue" because of the way it seems to be reaching down towards the streets below. But that name does absolutely no justice for this towering 34 foot statue that looms over 5th Avenue as if she was the city's guardian, ready to protect with her mighty trident in hand. Her real name is "Portlandia" and the Statue of Liberty is the only copper repousse statue larger than her in the country. She is definitely worth seeing, walk along 5th Avenue in between Main and Madison, and look to the skies. You won't miss her.

---- "What do teeth whitening, massage therapy, and an oxygen bar have in common?"
Da Vinci by Lien
555 SE 99th Avenue
Why would you want to just breathe the 21% oxygen air that we normally breathe all our life when you could be breathing a 90% oxygen laced with aromas such as eucalyptus, lavender, pina colada or vanilla? Fresh oxygen not for you? Well don't despair as you can always stop by to brush up your pearly whites with Da Vinci's teeth whitening services.

---- "This place sucks, but in a good way!"
Stark's Vacuums Museum
107 NE Grand Avenue
M-F 8a-7p and Sat 9a-4p
Considering this museum has over 300 vacuum cleaners on site, we would have to venture that this might have to be the cleanest building in the state. It's fascinating to see the progression over the years as well as the interesting design choices made in the past. There is even a vacuum that requires two people to operate it. The museum is just secondary though as this location if a fully functional Vacuum Cleaner sales and service business with top-notch merchandise for sale.

---- "I don't ever want to grow up."
Kidd Toy Museum
1301 SE Grand Avenue
This free museum is the result of a singular private citizen who had a passion for collecting... and sharing. The vast majority of the antiques/toys date back to the year 1869 until the year 1939, though there are still a collection of items from the newer generations. Just be aware that the title of the museum "Kidd" is based on the collector's name Kidd, not an indication that it is a child's museum. Some of the displays are even quite racist, but it's a good look into how some of the older generations saw the world, and shows just how far we have come as a nation.

---- "Not exactly the fountain of youth, but it will do."
Chimney Fountain
North of Southwest Lincoln
It's a fountain. That looks like a chimney. That's all you need to know, and if you get your kicks from seeking out fountains then you'll want to check out this red-bricked public one. It is actually quite interesting looking. The fountain is also referred to as the "Source Fountain" and it is one of the smallest fountains in the city.

---- "Why float on air when you could float on water..."
The Float Shoppe
1515 NW 23rd Avenue
If your body, mind, and soul all need a break at the same time then there might be no better place indoors in the Portland area than this. And if you have never "floated" before than you need to experience it at least once. The basic premise is that you drift away in a sensory deprivation atmosphere while lying in a salt infused pool of water which will result in you floating at the top without using any energy at all. The Float Shoppe gives you the option of using their revolutionary non-lid open floating tank if you are hesitant about submerging in the original fully closed floatrium.

---- "You got game right?"
Nike Portland
638 SW 5th Avenue
It's not just a store, it's an experience. Originally known as NikeTown, this sports institution moved its headquarters into the historic Kress building and renamed itself Nike Portland. These popular athletic shoes were actually invented in Oregon, so Portland seems like a natural place to showcase all the goods. The new headquarters comes complete with touch screen displays and replica bleachers.

---- "Where style meets comfort."
Living Room Theater
341 SW 10th Avenue
The Living Room Theater is your one stop date night extravaganza. There's a bar area, a European style café/restaurant, and of course the movie theater. But it's more than just a dinner and movie type of place. It is a sophisticated place for sophisticated adults. It is a place where you can drink a glass of wine (or a beer) while you watch a thought-provoking film on the big screen. Sure they show the occasional summer box office flick but the screens are usually packed with independent, foreign, and classic films. This is truly a Portland theater, as the creators had the environment in mind when designing this business. Natural materials and light were used to make it more energy conscious. The Living Room Theater is also the first all-digital and only-digital theater in the country, an earth friendly alternative to the chemicals and non-biodegradable products of normal movie theaters. Trying to save a little bit of money? Go to the theater on Monday or Tuesdays when they run specials for five dollars a movie ticket.

---- "Only true golfers can putt through the mouth of a clown."
Glowing Greens
509 SW Taylor Street
This company takes full advantage of its indoor miniature golf course. Glowing Greens has made miniature golfing even more fun than it already is by adding features such as 3D glasses and a glow-in-the-dark course. This is definitely one of the weirdest courses you will ever play. It's also a pirate-themed venture so dust off your old pirate Halloween costume and immerse yourself into this unusual experience.

---- "Many gyms are getting green over this new Green Gym."
The Green Microgym
1237 NE Alberta Street
Once again, the city of Portland has found a way to turn an ordinary business into a concept that just oozes with Portland characteristics. The most unique thing about these gyms is that the actual energy of the members, while they run on the treadmill, helps power the buildings through the use of electricity-generating equipment. Their green movement doesn't end there as they equip their studios with solar panels and low-flow toilets. The Green Microgym has a carbon footprint that is about ten percent of normal gyms.

---- "What is Room 529?"
Hotel Modera
515 SW Clay Street
The Modera may be one of the best rated hotels in the city of Portland, but that is not the reason it is included in this book. This reason is because of one of its particular rooms... Room 529. It's a collaborative space for the creative people of Portland to ascend and unite to create some magic. This room is set up to film all that takes place inside, and enough equipment to aid in the various photo shoots, music videos and live performances that have already taken place in this exciting new venture known simply as, Room 529.

---- "Where there is light, darkness is always creeping around the corner."
Shanghai Tunnels
Old Town/Chinatown
Located beneath the city of Portland are miles of tunnels and passageways that connect various buildings to the Willamette River. The purpose of these underground tunnels was to give businesses a faster and less populated avenue to moved goods/deliveries back and forth to the waterfront. But apparently that is not the only thing these tunnels were used for. There is a deep, dark myth shrouded here. For the story goes that these tunnels were used for "Shanghaiing." A practice involving nefarious groups of men snatching unsuspecting people from the streets and buildings and dragging them through the tunnels back to their ships where they would sell them into slavery or prostitution. Tours are now run to tell the history of these tunnels and take you through some of the basement areas connected with the tunnels.

---- "World's Largest Continual Chocolate Waterfall"

The Candy Basket

1924 NE 181st Avenue

Portland really seems to have a fascination with trying to get the record for the largest and/or smallest things in the world. The Candy Basket chocolate store boasts another one of the city's records as it house the "World's Largest Continual Chocolate Waterfall." Whether you think it looks like a waterfall, or rather more like a fountain, it makes no difference as this towering 20 foot chocolate heaven is a must see for anyone that claims to have a sweet tooth.

---- "The garden for people who aren't really into all that 'rose' stuff."

Japanese Garden

611 SW Kingston Avenue

There are plenty of cities in the country that boast their own Japanese Garden, but the reason we decided to add it to this book is because this garden is the king of the hill in the American market. This garden is proclaimed to be the most authentic Japanese garden outside of Japan. The Japanese Garden (nestled within Washington Park) is stunning in its simplicity and filled with a beautiful tranquility.

27. THE BEST OF THE REST – UNIQUE EVENTS AND FESTIVALS

---- "Jerimiah Johnson has nothing on this beauty."
West Coast Beard & Mustache Championships
1332 W Burnside Street
McMenamins Crystal Ballroom is home to a fierce yet majestic competition that showcases the finest facial hair throughout the land. Past competitors have ascended from far off places such as Pennsylvania and remote parts of Alaska. If you have a fascination for frontal hair styling or have an attraction for men who look like they have bears attached to their chins, then this is one event you do not want to miss.

---- "Who let the arghhs out?"
Portland Pirate Festival
St. Helens, Oregon
Labor Day Weekend can only mean one thing for Portland: the pirates will be pulling into harbor at the Columbia River. It's a festival filled with authentic pirate ships, battle shows, music & dance, markets, and yes plenty of sea-worthy attired pirates. This is a family oriented event that is not only fun, but quite educational. UPDATE: The 2013 Festival has been cancelled but there are already plans for the one in 2014 and the presenters are claiming it'll be the most extravagant festival yet to hit the high seas.

---- "Wait did you say Pub Crawl? Or Pug Crawl"
Portland Brewing Company Event
2730 NW 31st Avenue
This is indeed a Pug crawl as the Oregon Humane Society throws their annual Pug extravaganza through the streets of Portland. In May, come on down and squeal with delight as 100 to 500 costumed pugs show off their happiness for your viewing pleasure. Money raised from this event is used to help abandoned, abused and unwanted animals, not just pugs.

---- "How many pairs of pants are you wearing?"
Red Light's Annual CO-ED Naked Shopping Spree
3590 SE Hawthorne
Have you gotten your full share of nudity in Portland yet? Well if not then we've got another event for you that exhibits the free-spiritness of this Pacific Northwestern city. Contestants start out naked and then have a few minutes to run around the store while trying to put on the most clothes that they can. Even if you're not interested in the Naked Shopping Spree, you would still do wise to check out this locally owned store and perpetuate the meaning of "Keep Portland Weird." This spot was also voted as one of Portland's Favorite Vintage Stores.

---- "Just make sure you don't change the future…"
Pretend to be a Time Traveler Day
Northwest District
It's quite simple. On this day, you dress up as a character from the past or from the future, and act as if you are a time traveler. There are only a few rules you must abide by: You must spend the entire day in costume and character. And you cannot come out and directly tell anyone you are a time traveler, but you must show it through your actions and rhetoric. The official date is December 8th but recently people throughout the world have been opting to celebrate it in September to distance themselves from the massively popular holidays of late November/December.

---- "A full moon you say? Well bring out the gnomes!"
Lunar Gnome Roam
A group of Portland Gnome enthusiasts developed this tradition of dressing up as Gnomes and roaming around the city streets under the brightness of the full moon. They have also been known to throw lavish Gnome parties to celebrate these magical mythical beings. So if you are out in the streets of Portland on a full moon night, keep your eyes open for you might just see a group of ambling human-sized gnomes.

---- "It's only 36 degrees out you say? Well let's take off our pants!"

No Pants Day

January

This globally celebrated event takes place in the month of January and involves riding the public transit systems while wearing no pants. The Portland edition involves taking your pants off and riding through the city streets in the MAX and doing it with a completely straight face and pretending as if nothing is odd about all the people without pants. Afterwards there will be fun during some photo ops with your fellow travelers at the Pioneer Courthouse Square.

---- "May the fourth be with you…"

Star Wars Bar Crawl

If you haven't heard that phrase then you, my friend, are clearly not a nerd, and well, that's just too bad. The city of Portland realizes that even adults are nerds, so on May 4th they celebrate one of the grandest sci-fi franchises of all time, by dressing up as favorite characters from the flicks and going on a pub crawl through the downtown area. Whether you are part of the rebellion or tend to gravitate towards the dark side, you are still welcome.

---- "Make it so."

Captain Picard Day

2013 marks the third annual Captain Picard Day, where deep space nerds hyper-drive to the Floating World Comic store on Couch Street to honor the legendary captain of the Star Trek series. The walls are adorned with various representations of Picard by local admirers and artists. Trust us, you will see some bizarre pieces of art; and if you have any of your own you're welcome to enter it for free and for a chance to win prizes. It is also free to attend, and as with all Star Trek events, dressing up as your favorite character is encouraged.

28. THE BEST OF THE REST – UNIQUE PLACES TO GET YOUR GRUB ON

---- "Sprechen sie Deutsch?"

Rheinlander

5035 NE Sandy Blvd

You don't have to travel all the way to Germany to enjoy a little German food and German atmosphere. The Rheinlander restaurant is the Portland hotspot for anything German related. It's even worth a trip to just see the outside of the building. But if you decide to eat here then be ready for a splendorous feast featuring a culturally attired singing wait staff and authentic food and décor. And yes it comes complete with a German accordion player.

---- "World Famous Flaming Spanish Coffee Ceremony"

Huber's Café

411 SW 3rd Avenue

You did it! Congratulations on the World's Best cup of coffee. Okay that movie quote might not be entirely accurate in regards to this particular drink, but this could very well be the most interesting cup of coffee you will ever experience. The Spanish Coffee is mixed and poured tableside for your viewing pleasure, and yes it is complete with its own little fire show. Another interesting reason to check out this place: this is in fact the oldest restaurant for the city of Portland. It's been around since 1879! It's a fantastic place to travel back in time, especially if you sit back in the old vintage bar area.

---- "Who? What was the name of that doctor?"

The TARDIS Room

1218 N Killingsworth Street

Don't know what a TARDIS is? Well then you don't belong here. Kidding, but if you are a fan of British sci-fi or just a fan of fish and chips, then stop by the Fish and Chip Shop located on Killingsworth Street. And yes the front door is a TARDIS, and the bathroom door is a TARDIS as well.

---- **"I like my kava stirred, not shaken."**
Bula Kava House
3115 SE Division Street
The only Kava bar in Portland. What is kava? Some people say it's a substance straight from heaven. Others say it's the solution to all their problems. You be the judge yourself and pull up chair to see what all the fuss is about. It is a great atmosphere, and the staff is more than willing to give you a history lesson on this rare plant that is most commonly compared to alcohol.

---- **"Is it getting hot in here?"**
Salvador Molly's Great Balls of Fire
1523 SW Sunset Blvd
Are you looking for a food challenge? Then step into Salvador Molly's and take their Great Balls of Fire challenge. These fiery little bad boys have made appearances on some of television's elite food shows. Also, for 17 years running now, Salvador Molly's has also used their Great Balls of Fire to help out the community by having a fundraiser. For every Great Ball of Fire eaten they donate money to an organization that helps low-income Oregon households pay their utility bills. They've raised over $45,000 for the non-profit organization. Salvador Molly's initially began as a simple food cart but has grown into a true and popular local Portland cafe. "Keep Portland Weird" by supporting this local and community driven eatery.

---- **"Is our waitress looking a little pale to you?"**
Old Town Pizza
226 NW Davis Street
If you want to go ghost hunting then one of the haunted hotspots in Portland that you will want to check out is the Old Town Pizza. This downtown eatery is haunted by a century old prostitute and has been seen by numerous employees and guests. But besides the ghost, this is still a great place to have a pizza and beer. They have several rooms to sit in at your leisure, all filled with its own unique décor and antique seating items.

29. THE BEST OF THE REST – MISC. ITEMS THAT DON'T QUITE FIT

---- "Who you gonna call…"
UFO Response Team
Well it's not ghosts, so you don't need to call that famous foursome, but if you happen to run into any aliens then the UFO Response Team may be the first form of specialists you should contact. This privately funded organization operates all up and down the west coast, and seeks out individuals who have had experiences with unidentified flying objects. You can spot them driving in the white or black cruisers with the words "UFO RESPONSE TEAM" printed boldly on the trunk of the vehicle.

--- "And so it has begun."
Yarn Bombing
The seedy underbelly of the Portland youth has reared its head in the form of a new style of graffiti that is attacking the city streets. Okay actually that's a little bit of an overstatement. Yes there is a new wave of graffiti sweeping the city but it's in the form of a unity of knitters. Yes knitters. With yarn and such. So if you spot a bike rack or telephone pole wrapped in tightly wound yarn, then you will finally be able to witness this intense new form of vandalism. But hey it looks pretty!

---- "How many bears are in the city of Portland?"
Animals in Pools
555 SW Yamhill Street
You don't have to pay the admission to the zoo to see some bears, otters, and seals. Just walk east down the streets closest to the Pioneer Courthouse Square to find a perfect photo opportunity to hang out with some animals by the pool. Granted they are just copper renditions of the animals, but hey that makes it a lot easier to wrap your arms around them and kiss them while you pose for the camera.

---- **"It's not all just horseplay you know…"**
Chained up Plastic Horses
NW 23rd Avenue
Couch and 9th Street
The Northwestern part of the city still has metal rings located throughout the sides of the streets. In the past, these rings were used to tie down real life horses, but with the advent of the automobile these poor rings lost their purpose for life and were left to spend the rest of their days in a lonely and quiet sadness. But do not despair! In a show of true compassion, the citizens of Portland took it upon themselves to use some wire and string to tie little plastic horses onto the rings. The rings shine brightly now with having been given back a purpose for life.

---- **"No one is cutting down this tree! Well unless we score a goal…"**
Timbers Army
1844 SW Morrison Street
Only in soccer would a group of hundreds sing and chant nonstop through the entirety of a sports event. This rowdy group of individuals (called the Timbers Army) is the hardcore cheering squad of the Portland Timbers soccer team. Each game they rock the stadium with their waving flags, inspired song lyrics, green smoke, and a lumberjack who chainsaws a piece of a log off after every time the Timbers score. Your best bet would be to go to a game when they play Seattle, their archrivals and most hated opponent. The stadium will be rocking.

---- **"Let's get our drink on! Agua style!"**
Benson Bubblers
Fifty throughout the city
There's plenty of water in the city of Portland and I'm not just talking about all the rain. For 365 days, 17 hours a day, water runs freely through the 50-some water fountains strategically placed throughout the city. These are the Benson Bubblers and they are an iconic piece of Portland lore, a fresh unique addition to a unique city. The water is always fresh and constantly erupting water so no need to touch the actual bowls if you are afraid of germs.

---- "I would walk a thousand miles... okay no maybe more like ten miles."

Portland Walking Tours

If you are visiting Portland then get ready because you are going to be doing a lot of walking. The roads are narrow, the parking is scarce, but don't stress as this is the best way to truly experience the city and its diversity. And since you're already going to be walking, you might as well sign up for one of the Portland Walking Tours. USA Today referred to the Portland Walking Tours as one of the top five walking tours in the nation. Critics love these tours and if you check out the reviews online, so does all the visitors to Portland. Even if you've lived in Portland all your life, this is one tour you need to check out as many people claim that they always learn something new. They have seven different tours to choose from.

---- "Is it just me or are you awesome?"

March Fourth Marching Band

Portland's best local band doesn't hold back any punches in its display of musical fortitude that comes complete with stilt walkers and fire/flag dancers. This marching band style musical group inspires its audience with its jovial musical celebrations with its marching band themed costumes and instrumental brass band music.

---- "Beam me up Portland."

Portland by Segway

150 SW Harrison Street

Okay so Segways are not exactly "sci-fi," but you will still have a blast and feel as if you are in a futuristic world sent back in time to take a tour of the vintage folk using their feet to get around town. This tour takes you through the bustling streets of the downtown area with stops at many of the city's well known landmarks, all while riding a Segway.

---- "Are you ready to rumble?!"

Stray Boots

Downtown Portland

If a simple walking tour isn't interactive enough for you, then you should try out the craze that is sweeping the nation. It's an urban adventure that uses the capabilities of your phone or smart device to send you on a journey through the city for a scavenger hunt. It's educational genius that involves using clues and games to help take you on an adventurous self-guided tour of the city.

---- **"There is a place where you can find your other half…"**

Glove Tree

Alberta Street

What exactly is a glove tree? It's a lost and found for mittens and gloves of all shapes, sizes, and colors. Hanging from the tree they wait in quiet desperation for their other half to be returned to them and make them whole and complete once again. So if you have any gloves that have no mate or find a singular one on the streets of Portland, head on over to Alberta Street and maybe, just maybe you'll be able to complete a pair.

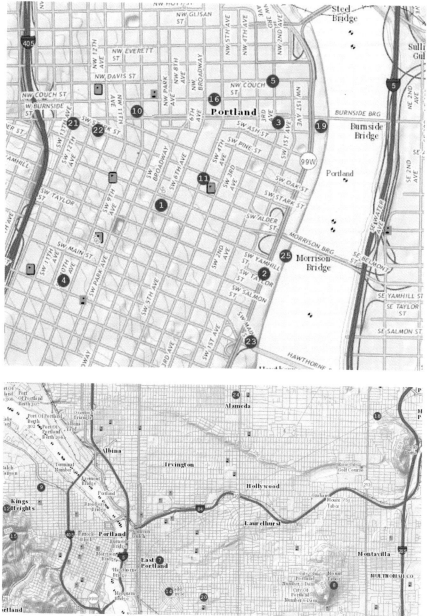

Credit: U.S. Geological Survey; Department of the Interior/USGS

Made in the USA
Lexington, KY
07 June 2014